A TRUE BOOK

T0053796

Geothermal Energy

The Energy Inside Our Planet

LAURIE BREARLEY

Children's Press®
An Imprint of Scholastic Inc.

Content Consultant
Kevin Doran, J.D., Institute Fellow and Research Professor,
Renewable and Sustainable Energy Institute,
University of Colorado at Boulder

Library of Congress Cataloging-in-Publication Data

Names: Brearley, Laurie, 1953- author.
Title: Geothermal energy : the energy inside our planet / by Laurie Brearley.
Other titles: True book.
Description: New York, NY : Children's Press, [2018] | Series: A true book |
    Includes bibliographical references and index.
Identifiers: LCCN 2018009073| ISBN 9780531236857 (library binding) | ISBN
    9780531239421 (pbk.)
Subjects: LCSH: Geothermal resources--Juvenile literature. | Geothermal power
    plants--Juvenile literature.
Classification: LCC GB1199.5 .B74 2018 | DDC 333.8/8--dc23 LC record available at
    https://lccn.loc.gov/2018009073

All rights reserved. Published in 2019 by Children's Press, an imprint of Scholastic Inc.
Printed in Heshan, China 62

SCHOLASTIC, CHILDREN'S PRESS, A TRUE BOOK™, and associated logos are trademarks and/or
registered trademarks of Scholastic Inc.

Scholastic Inc., 557 Broadway, New York, NY 10012

1 2 3 4 5 6 7 8 9 10 R 28 27 26 25 24 23 22 21 20 19

Front cover: An eruption at Mount Etna
Back cover: Stokkur geyser in Iceland

Find the Truth!

Everything you are about to read is true *except* for one of the sentences on this page.

Which one is **TRUE**?

T or F   About 10 percent of Iceland's energy comes from geothermal sources.

T or F   Earth's inner core can reach temperatures of 12,600 degrees Fahrenheit (7,000 degrees Celsius).

Find the answers in this book.

Contents

THE **BIG** TRUTH!

Sharing the Wealth

Earth's layers

4

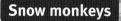
Snow monkeys

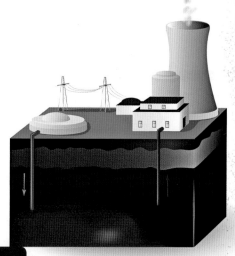
Geothermal power plant

5

A Need for Alternative Energy

We use energy every day. It fuels cars and powers cell phones. It cools homes when it's hot outside and warms them when the weather turns cold. It provides light through the night while the sun shines on the other half of the world.

All this energy must come from somewhere. For centuries, people have relied mostly on fossil fuels such as coal, oil, and natural gas. These materials burn easily to create heat and can be turned into electricity. But they are far from perfect.

Our supply of fossil fuels is limited. Experts predict that **fossil fuels will dwindle and their cost will rise**. In addition, **burning these fuels releases harmful substances**. Some substances trap heat within the atmosphere, leading to **climate change**. Others cause health problems, including heart and lung diseases.

What Can We Do?

Renewable energy sources, such as solar, wind, water, and geothermal, are healthier sources than fossil fuels. They can serve our electricity needs while reducing the damage done to the planet and us.

Turn the page to learn about the power inside our planet: geothermal energy.

Old Faithful shoots boiling
water up to 185 feet
(56 meters) into the air.

CHAPTER 1

Earth's Heat

Visitors to Yellowstone National Park ooh and aah as they watch Old Faithful, the park's most famous **geyser**. About once every hour, the geyser shoots thousands of gallons of hot water into the air. As soon as the colossal jet of water stops, steam spews out with a thundering roar. Old Faithful has been erupting in this way for more than 100 years. What causes this fantastic show? Geothermal energy.

Energy From Earth

The word *geothermal* comes from two Greek words: *geo*, or "earth," and *thermes*, which means "heat." Geothermal energy is the heat found deep within the earth. Scientists are interested in using this type of energy because it is renewable. That means it never runs out! The planet is continuously producing geothermal energy.

A scientist takes measurements near Bardarbunga Volcano in Iceland.

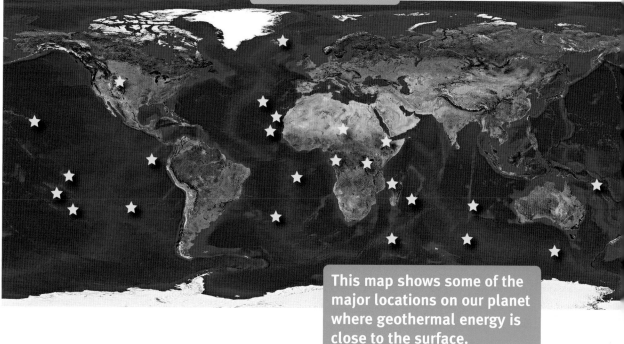

This map shows some of the major locations on our planet where geothermal energy is close to the surface.

Geothermal energy exists all around the world. In many parts of the world, it is located too deep within the planet for us to reach. But there are some areas where the heat is very close to the surface. Here, not only is it easy to access, but it sometimes comes spilling out of the surface all on its own. This is especially true in places such as Iceland and the western United States.

Thermal Features

Geothermal heat escapes from underground in many ways. One of the most dangerous is a volcano. A volcano is a vent in Earth's surface. **Magma**, or melted rock, flows up from deep below and collects in pools, or **reservoirs**, beneath the planet's crust. This magma escapes as lava through volcanoes. Hot gases, ash, and fragments of hot rock may also erupt. These substances might shoot out with tons of force, or they might slowly ooze.

Kilauea, a volcano in Hawaii, is almost always erupting.

Earth's Layers

Earth has four basic layers: the crust, the mantle, the outer core, and the inner core. Temperatures are hottest in the inner core. This heat moves outward through the outer core and the mantle to the crust.

Earth's crust is not solid. It is broken into several pieces called **tectonic plates**. These plates push, pull, and slide against one another. Geothermal energy is easiest to reach where two plates meet, especially if those plates are pulling apart.

CRUST
Rigid rock broken into tectonic plates

MANTLE
1,800° to 6,700°F
(1,000° to 3,700°C)
Soft, flexible rock

OUTER CORE
7,200° to 9,000°F
(4,000° to 5,000°C)
Liquid iron

INNER CORE
9,000° to 12,600°F
(5,000° to 7,000°C)
Solid iron

Tiny organisms living in hot springs (like this) and mudpots can turn these hydrothermal features a range of colors.

Mudpot

When geothermal energy combines with water, it creates **hydrothermal** features. One example is a hot spring. A spring is any opening through which underground water reaches the surface. In hot springs, the water is warmed by magma or other deep heat sources.

A mudpot is a type of hot spring filled with mud. Heat from underground water warms pools of water on the surface. The surface water mixes with clay, creating mud. Gas and steam escape from deep below, making mudpots bubble and boil.

A fumarole is a steam vent. Fumaroles have little water, and it boils to steam before reaching the surface. The steam shoots out at temperatures as hot as 280 degrees Fahrenheit (138 degrees Celsius). Sometimes, fumaroles hiss or whistle, just like a teakettle.

Geysers, such as Old Faithful in Yellowstone National Park, are similar to hot springs, but the flow of water is partly blocked. Pressure builds up underground until it pushes steam and water up to the surface. The escaping steam and water can shoot high into the air.

The steam from some fumaroles contains toxic gases from deep underground.

About 95 percent of the buildings in Reykjavik, Iceland, are connected to a geothermal heating system.

CHAPTER 2

Power from the Planet

For thousands of years, people have harnessed geothermal heat. Its age-old uses range from housework to recreation. Some people buried food such as bread dough to cook it, as in an oven. Others used the hot water in natural springs to wash clothes. Today, power plants turn that energy into electricity to power everything from computers to nightlights. Some types of geothermal energy can even directly heat a building.

Ancient Heat

Native Americans first used hot springs at least 10,000 years ago. The warm, mineral-rich waters cooked food and helped ease the aches and pains of bathers. In China, emperors built palaces around hot springs, where the leaders bathed, before the third century BCE. Roman troops invaded Britain in the first century CE. They built bathhouses in Bath, England, that still attract visitors today.

Timeline of Geothermal Energy Use

1000s BCE
Emperors first bathe in the Huaqing hot springs in China.

| 8000 BCE | 1000s BCE | 60 CE |

8000 BCE
Native Americans use hot springs for cooking and health.

60 CE
Romans in Britain build Bath's first bathhouses.

New developments occurred in the 20th century. Italian inventor Piero Conti built the world's first geothermal **generator** in 1904. This meant geothermal energy could be used to create electricity. By 1913, Conti had constructed a power plant at Larderello, Italy. The United States built its first geothermal power plant in 1922 in California. Reykjavik, Iceland, began using geothermal energy to heat buildings in 1930.

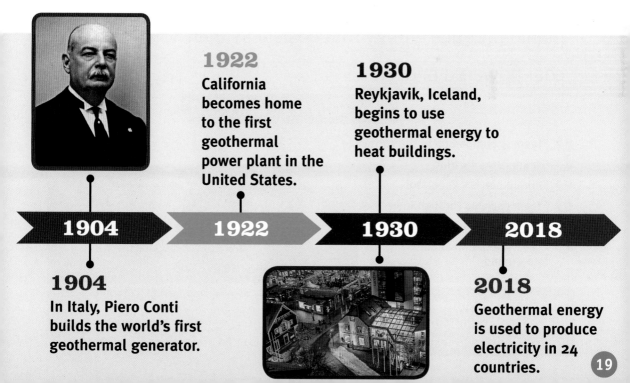

1922
California becomes home to the first geothermal power plant in the United States.

1930
Reykjavik, Iceland, begins to use geothermal energy to heat buildings.

1904 — **1922** — **1930** — **2018**

1904
In Italy, Piero Conti builds the world's first geothermal generator.

2018
Geothermal energy is used to produce electricity in 24 countries.

From Steam to Electricity

Traditional power plants burn fossil fuels such as coal to heat water and produce steam. This steam turns **turbines** that drive generators to produce electricity. Geothermal power plants do not need fossil fuels. They are built near natural geothermal reservoirs and use Earth's steam to turn turbines. The steam is created from underground water sources for free and without human assistance. As a result, geothermal plants produce energy that costs less than coal-powered energy.

GEOTHERMAL POWER PLANT

1. Steam is pumped up to the surface.
2. Steam turns turbine
3. Turbine powers generator
4. Steam escapes through towers
5. Used water cools in reservoir
6. Cool water pumped back into ground

This diagram shows the basic workings of a geothermal power plant.

To bring the steam to the surface, workers drill wells into the earth's crust. Steam collects in these wells and is pushed up through turbines that drive generators.

One of the world's largest geothermal reservoirs is beneath

A group of geothermal power plants known as The Geysers is located in the Mayacamas Mountains.

The Geysers in northern California. The Geysers is a complex of 22 geothermal power plants. These plants have successfully produced a steady supply of geothermal electricity since the 1960s. They power most of northern California!

At mudpots, hot water and steam are both released to the surface by geothermal activity.

Power from Hot Water

Most geothermal reservoirs release hot water in addition to steam. Many power plants only use the steam to produce electricity. They pipe the hot water back into the reservoir. That water, however, can be used to produce electricity, too. This is especially useful where the water is not hot enough to produce steam. Two methods are used to turn hot water into electricity. One is called binary cycle. The other is total flow.

At geothermal plants that use the binary cycle, geothermal hot water heats other liquids that boil at lower temperatures. These liquids boil and create steam, which drives turbines.

In total flow, hot water is forced through special nozzles that turn it into high-pressure jets. The powerful jets then turn turbines.

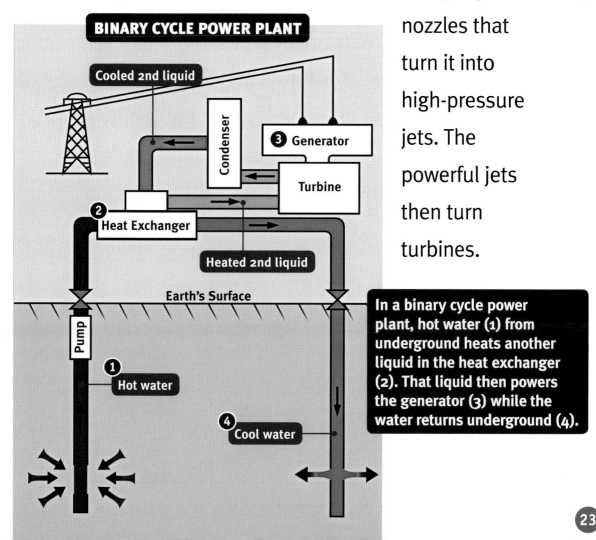

BINARY CYCLE POWER PLANT

Cooled 2nd liquid

Condenser

3 Generator

Turbine

2
Heat Exchanger

Heated 2nd liquid

Earth's Surface

Pump

1
Hot water

4
Cool water

In a binary cycle power plant, hot water (1) from underground heats another liquid in the heat exchanger (2). That liquid then powers the generator (3) while the water returns underground (4).

Heat from Hot Water

Geothermal energy does not need to be turned into electricity to be useful. It can also heat buildings— whether a school, an office, or a home—directly. To do this, hot water from geothermal sources is pumped through a network of pipes into buildings. The water's heat radiates into a building's rooms, keeping them warm. In Iceland, which has plenty of heat available at or near the surface, this is the most common method of heating.

Water in a geothermal heating system not only heats the air, but can also provide hot water for faucets.

Radiators

Control panel

Showers, baths, . . .

Taps

Water

Tank

Pump

Boiler

Black egg

This type of heating can drive industry, as well. Some greenhouses and livestock farms in Russia and Italy rely on heat from geothermal hot water. In Japan, fish farms use it to keep water warm for shellfish, tropical fish, and catfish. It can also help dry wood and fabric. In the food industry, such systems help **pasteurize** milk and dehydrate—or pull the moisture from—fruits and vegetables. Geothermal heat can even purify the soil so mushrooms can thrive!

Heat from the Ground

Tapping into geothermal heat does not always require deep wells. Just below Earth's surface, the temperature remains a constant 55°F (13°C) all year. This may not sound very warm, but it is enough to keep a home comfortable. This

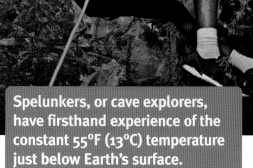

Spelunkers, or cave explorers, have firsthand experience of the constant 55°F (13°C) temperature just below Earth's surface.

underground warmth is called ground-sourced heat.

Special systems can take advantage of ground-sourced heat. A network of pipes loops from a house to a heat pump, into the ground, and back again.

Water circulates through the pipe network. During the winter, the water absorbs heat from the ground. As it flows through the heat pump, the heat is concentrated and sent as warm air throughout the home.

The system works in reverse in summer. The water absorbs heat from the house. It cools as it passes underground and then flows to the heat pump. There, the cooler temperatures are concentrated to create air-conditioning.

Geothermal heat near Earth's surface only reaches a temperature of about 55°F (13°C), but that is much warmer than the winter temperatures in many northern climates.

Sharing the Wealth

Can countries share energy with each other? Iceland sits on top of a boundary where two tectonic plates meet. It is home to hot springs, volcanoes, and plenty of geothermal energy. The country also uses water, wind, and solar power. Other countries, such as its neighbor the United Kingdom, still struggle to cut down on fossil fuels. Through the coming decades, developers plan to build a connection of underwater cables between Iceland and the United Kingdom. This connection, called the IceLink, would allow electricity to flow between the countries. But how will this incredible technology work?

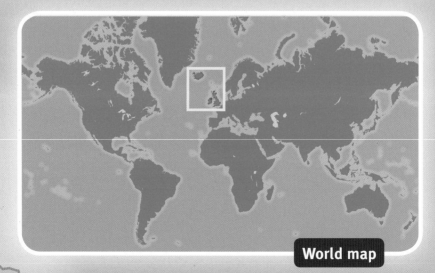

World map

Iceland

- As of 2015, 97 percent of all heat used is geothermal.
- 26 percent of electricity is geothermal.
- Only 0.02 percent of electricity and 2.7 percent of heat comes from oil or other sources.
- Iceland may be able to produce significantly more clean energy than it needs.

ICELAND

IceLink

- The IceLink would be an interconnector. This is a connection between countries that carries electricity or other energy back and forth.
- This would allow Iceland to send extra electricity to the United Kingdom.
- Officials have been discussing building the IceLink for more than 60 years.
- Researchers currently estimate the IceLink could be usable by 2027.
- Construction costs are estimated to be more than $3.5 billion.
- The IceLink would be the longest interconnector in the world at more than 620 miles (998 kilometers).

United Kingdom

- As of 2016, 81.5 percent of all energy comes from oil and other fossil fuels.
- Roughly 9 percent of all energy comes from renewable sources.
- Geothermal energy is slightly more than 1 percent of all renewable energy.
- The country hopes to have 15 percent of its energy come from renewable sources by 2020. Bringing clean energy in from other places can help the country reach this goal.

IRELAND

UNITED KINGDOM

Nevada is second only to California in U.S. geothermal energy production.

CHAPTER 3

Tracking the Heat

To use geothermal resources, we first have to find them. People look for the heat of geothermal reservoirs hidden underground. These reservoirs contain hot water or steam trapped in cracks or other spaces underground. For the most accurate temperature measurements, researchers dig wells 60 to 300 feet (18 to 91 m) into the ground. Digging, however, is costly and time-consuming. So researchers use a variety of tools to help them decide where to drill.

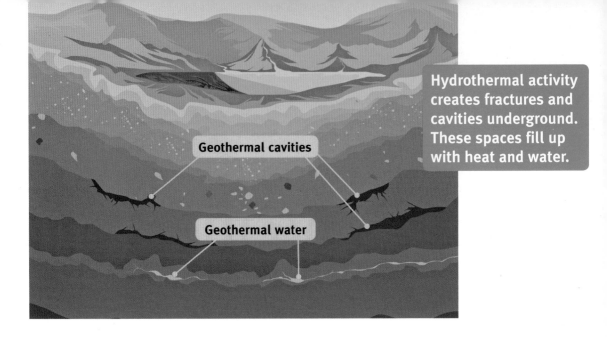

Geothermal cavities

Geothermal water

Hydrothermal activity creates fractures and cavities underground. These spaces fill up with heat and water.

An Electric Charge

In the past, most geothermal exploration took place near hot springs and other features. Today, however, researchers have other methods to help them find geothermal reservoirs. One of these is electricity. The heat, water, and fractures that accompany hydrothermal features all help turn rocks into better **conductors**. Researchers send electrical currents into the ground. If the rocks below conduct electricity well, the area likely has some geothermal activity.

Picturing the Underground

Gravity **surveys** measure and map the density of the ground below the surface. This gives researchers an idea of what types of rocks and features lie underground. Surveyors look for low-density areas, which can indicate water, fractures, and other features.

Magnets offer another peek underground. When minerals reach a certain temperature, they lose any magnetism they had. Finding areas with little or no magnetism can indicate high temperatures and geothermal activity.

A gravimeter is a tool that allows researchers to test the gravity in an area.

Testing the Waters

Chemistry also helps test for a usable geothermal source. Researchers take samples of water, steam, and gases. They test for minerals such as sulfur and sodium, and check the acid level of the sample. This helps researchers estimate the temperature and depth of geothermal reservoirs.

Soil samples also offer clues. Hydrothermal features often add carbon dioxide and mercury to the soil. If the soil has high levels of those elements, the area is a promising geothermal source.

Swimming in Winter

Geothermal activity is a great find for humans looking to power their homes. It is a treat for other animals, too! Japanese macaques, also called snow monkeys, are a famous example.

One population of macaques lives in Joshin'etsukogen National Park, which has a lot of hydrothermal activity. In winter, they stay warm in the hot springs. They bathe, play, and groom one another.

Piton de la Fournaise on Réunion Island in the Indian Ocean is one of the world's most active volcanoes.

A scientist takes a lava sample from Piton de la Fournaise volcano on Réunion Island.

CHAPTER 4

A Geothermal Future

Today, geothermal energy supplies less than 1 percent of the world's electricity. This energy relies on the steam and hot water that naturally occur in hydrothermal features. But not all geothermal features are wet. We haven't been able to tap the energies of hot, dry rock or of magma. If we could find a way to turn their heat into electricity, our supply of renewable energy would skyrocket.

Just Add Water

Some 2.5 miles (4 km) beneath Earth's surface, rocks heat to more than 464°F (240°C). This hot, dry rock represents the world's largest potential source of geothermal energy. Because the rock is dry, however, there is no natural steam or water to run turbines. For a long time, people did not have the technology necessary to use this energy source. This is changing with the Enhanced Geothermal System (EGS).

The EGS power plant at Soultz-sous-Forêts in France began as a facility just for research. It started producing and selling electricity in 2015.

With EGS, drillers dig two wells deep into the hot rock. Water is pumped at high pressure into one well. The hot rock heats the water, which is then pumped up through the second well. As it reaches the surface, the hot water turns to steam. The steam runs turbines and generates electricity. Then the water is pumped back down for reuse.

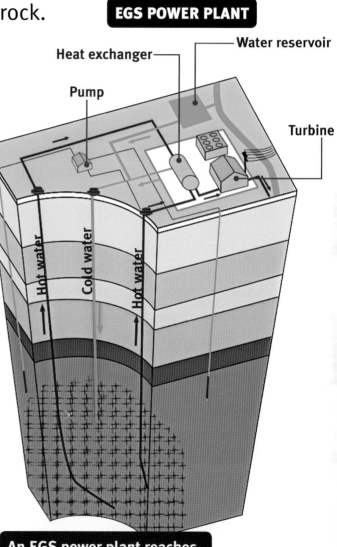

EGS POWER PLANT

Water reservoir

Heat exchanger

Pump

Turbine

Hot water

Cold water

Hot water

An EGS power plant reaches deeper into the earth than other forms of geothermal power production.

Magma

Magma, or molten rock, is an even more powerful source than hot, dry rock. This superheated liquid holds a lot of energy. It can heat water to 1,000°F (538°C) or more. A project in Iceland is currently working to drill miles into the earth to reach magma and capture its energy. It is still in the early stages, and many organizations around the world are contributing to the research.

At geothermal facilities like this one in Iceland, experts are still searching for the safest and most efficient way to drill miles into the earth.

HÆTTA
Vinsamlega yfirgefið svæðið
ef neyðarflauta borsins
er virkjuð

ATTENTION
In case of emergency
Please evacuate area
if drill rig alarm is activated

The Danakil Depression in Ethiopia is a hotbed of geothermal activity. Volcanoes, hot springs, and even a lava lake are found there.

Today and Tomorrow

Today, geothermal energy heats buildings in 72 countries and produces electricity in 24. Yet this energy accounts for the tiniest fraction of the world's power needs. Still, the outlook is changing. New technology is making geothermal energy more efficient and accessible. Experts predict that geothermal sources will supply 3.5 percent of our energy by 2050. Even this small amount can make a big difference in our renewable energy options and the health of our planet. ★

Looking Back at the Book

What have you learned? Here's a quick review!
Can you add any details to the bits and pieces below?

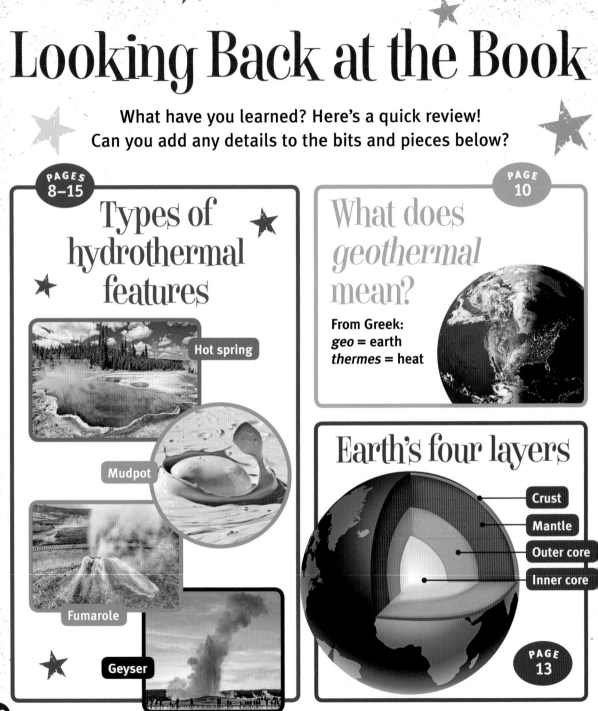

PAGES 8–15

Types of hydrothermal features

Hot spring

Mudpot

Fumarole

Geyser

PAGE 10

What does *geothermal* mean?

From Greek:
geo = earth
thermes = heat

Earth's four layers

Crust

Mantle

Outer core

Inner core

PAGE 13

Current uses of geothermal energy

PAGES 20–27

★ **Generating electricity**

★ **Heating buildings**

★ **Heating water at fish farms**

★ **Pasteurizing milk**

★ **Purifying soil**

★ **Dehydrating fruits and vegetables**

Ways to find potential geothermal energy sources

PAGES 31–34

★ **Measuring temperature underground**
★ **Electrical currents**

★ **Gravity surveys (above)**
★ **Magnetic studies**

★ **Water, steam, gas, and soil chemistry (above)**

New geothermal energy technologies

PAGES 36–40

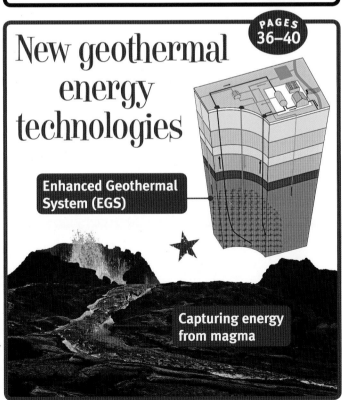

Enhanced Geothermal System (EGS)

Capturing energy from magma

Number of geysers in Yellowstone National Park: About 300

Number of countries with geothermal power plants: 24

Percent of the United States' electricity that comes from geothermal sources: 0.3

Number of fossil fuels involved in geothermal electricity production: 0

Times per day Old Faithful erupts: 12 to 24

Did you find the truth?

F About 10 percent of Iceland's energy comes from geothermal sources.

T Earth's inner core can reach temperatures of 12,600 degrees Fahrenheit (7,000 degrees Celsius).

Resources

Books

Brennan, Linda Crotta. *Geothermal Power*. Ann Arbor, MI: Cherry Lake Publishing, 2013.

Rowell, Rebecca. *Energy and Waves Through Infographics*. Minneapolis: Lerner Publications Company, 2014.

Sneideman, Joshua. *Renewable Energy: Discover the Fuel of the Future with 20 Projects*. White River Junction, VT: Nomad Press, 2016.

Visit this Scholastic website for more information on Geothermal Energy:

★ www.factsfornow.scholastic.com
Enter the keywords **Geothermal Energy**

Important Words

climate change (KLYE-mit CHAYNJ) global warming and other changes in the weather and weather patterns that are happening because of human activity

conductors (kuhn-DUHK-turz) substances that allow heat, electricity, or sound to travel through

generator (JEN-uh-ray-tur) a machine that produces electricity by turning a magnet inside a coil of wire

geyser (GYE-zur) underground hot spring that shoots boiling water and steam into the air

hydrothermal (hye-druh-THUR-muhl) of or relating to hot water

magma (MAG-muh) melted rock found beneath Earth's surface that becomes lava when it flows out of volcanoes

pasteurize (PAS-chuh-rize) to heat milk or another liquid to a temperature that is high enough to kill harmful bacteria

reservoirs (REZ-ur-vwahrz) natural or artificial lakes or pools where water is stored

surveys (SUR-vayz) studies of the lines and angles of a piece of land in order to make a map or plan

tectonic plates (tek-TAH-nik PLAYTS) the sections of Earth's outer layer that float on the mantle

turbines (TUR-buhnz) engines powered by water, steam, wind, or gas passing through the blades of a wheel and making it spin

Index

Page numbers in **bold** indicate illustrations.

About the Author

Laurie Brearley has written and edited numerous children's books and articles on a wide range of topics in science and social studies. She holds degrees from the University of New Hampshire and Boston University. Brearley believes that learning is a lifelong pursuit. She currently lives in Binghamton, New York, and is proud to be a descendant of David Brearley, one of the signers of the U.S. Constitution.